THE MARITAL COMPATIBILITY TEST

THE MARITAL COMPATIBILITY TEST

Hundreds of Questions for Couples to Answer Together

Susan Adams

A CITADEL PRESS BOOK
Published by Carol Publishing Group

A Citadel Press Book
Published by Carol Publishing Group
Citadel Press is a registered trademark of Carol Communications, Inc.
Editorial Offices: 600 Madison Avenue, New York, N.Y. 10022
Sales and Distribution Offices: 120 Enterprise Avenue, Secaucus, N.J. 07094
In Canada: Canadian Manda Group, One Atlantic Avenue, Suite 105, Toronto, Ontario M6K 3E7
Queries regarding rights and permissions should be addressed to Carol Publishing Group, 600 Madison Avenue, New York, N.Y. 10022

Carol Publishing Group books are available at special discounts for bulk purchases, for sales promotions, fund-raising, or educational purposes. Special editions can be created to specifications. For details, contact Special Sales Department, Carol Publishing Group, 120 Enterprise Avenue, Secaucus, N.J. 07094

Manufactured in the United States of America
10 9 8 7 6 5 4 3 2 1

Library of Congress Cataloging-in-Publication Data
Adams, Susan (Susan A.)
    The marital compatibility test: hundreds of questions for couples to answer together / Susan Adams.
        p.   cm.
    "A Citadel Press book."
    ISBN 0-8065-1634-8 (pbk.)
    1. Mate selection—United States.   2. Marriage—United States.
3. Marriage compatibility tests—United States.   I. Title.
HO801.A514   1995
646.7'7—dc20   94-25218
                                                      CIP

CONTENTS

INTRODUCTION

Before You Say "I Do"

Getting married! Excited, huh? At this very moment you may be planning a big church wedding or a simple ceremony at the courthouse. Maybe an afternoon garden wedding. (I've tried all three.) Whatever you're planning right now, it probably isn't divorce. But as we all know from those who are so free with their grim statistics, or rather, *our* grim statistics, a trip to the altar does not a life of wedded bliss make.

Anyone who has planned a wedding knows the event can take on a life of its own. Wondering, as you drift off to sleep, about the Dow or the Tao is replaced by worrying about the availability of fresh baby's breath in January and the color of the groom's cummerbund.

Yes, getting married is no piece of cake; in fact, it's downright scary. The only thing more frightening than getting married is *being* married. Once the euphoria wears off after the honeymoon, it dawns on you that you have just signed a major contract with no "buyer's remorse" clause. You have just begun a fifty-year "date" with no chance of saying at the door, "I'll call you in a few days," knowing you won't. Your date's door is *your* door—forever.

Mine is a voice from the trenches. Married three times, I am considerably wiser now than I was in 1969 when I first walked down the aisle on my father's arm to the theme from *Romeo and Juliet*. Since then, I have never forgotten an argument's source, major points, or its outcome. This is not to say I hold grudges or bear ill will. Not at all. It's just that marital bickering and spatting is often over such petty things that they're easy to remember.

Certainly, friendly disagreement and compromise are parts of every marriage, but I believe few people realize how much compromise and change may be necessary to make their marriage a stable one. I offer these quizzes as sources of premarital discussion: a means of heading off divorce at the pre-blood-test stage. There are no right answers or wrong answers, only responses that will speak for themselves and for your future.

All of this talk of marital misery may sound like a real "downer." After all, it seems as if I'm throwing cold water on a wonderful and joyous event—your wedding. But look at these quizzes and the discussions that will follow as life insurance. Insurance that you really know what you're getting and that it will be great for both of you.

Divorces for the most part are horrible, soul-shaking events. Foreign or domestic, they make you question your own value and sanity. They may look easy on the outside, but rarely is there calm at the eye of the storm. Regaining peace of mind is usually a long, painful, costly effort. So for your own sakes, for your parents' sakes, for your future children's sakes, take these quizzes and talk about the results. If you have to, fight about the results. You may find that, indeed, you both approach life in pretty much the same way and that yours is a union made in heaven. Or you may find you disagree on everything from doing the den in Early American to buying only dry dog food for Fido.

If you're still thinking, "Why rock the boat by taking these quizzes?" I understand. That's what I thought when warning flags went up in my mind a few weeks before I married for the first time. I was sorry I hadn't followed my intuition. So take heart and do it. To be in love is great, but to know chances are good you'll be staying in love is even greater.

AUTHOR'S NOTE

Lest you think I have incredible gall, writing a book such as this after the rise and fall of three marriages, let me explain. The quizzes you are about to take were written for my daughter, Alyson, in an attempt to provide her with a rare combination of fun and insight—a painless way for her to gain a little wisdom in choosing a life's mate. She and others have enjoyed and appreciated the tests so much, they have encouraged me to offer them to you who may benefit from my marital missteps. May these quizzes confirm that you have much in common, that you can compromise when you don't, and that the future holds a lifetime of love for both of you.

THE MARITAL COMPATIBILITY TEST

1 RUDE FOOD: TWINKIES OR TOFU?

Chocoholics definitely have more fun, don't they? If that statement just got your sprouts and bean curd in an uproar, great—unless you're marrying a closet chocoholic. During courtship many people don't feel comfortable revealing their eating idiosyncrasies. After you are married, you may find that spouse's mashed-banana-and-peanut-butter sandwich stimulates your own culinary creativity. Or you may find that the sight of it makes you physically ill. Try living with a person who eats apples over the sink so he can spit out the skin and pulp! *Bon appétit!*

1. <u>My</u> idea of a great snack is
   a. chips and dip.
   b. fruit and cheese.
   c. ice cream.
   d. fresh raw vegetables.
   e. Twinkies and Ring-Dings.
   f. unsalted popcorn.
   g. other _____

2. When people criticize my eating habits, I
   a. want to slap them but don't.
   b. want to slap them and do.
   c. appreciate their concern.
   d. ignore them.
   e. change my habits, at least for the moment.

3. Eating in bed is
   a. the eighth deadly sin.
   b. deliciously decadent.
   c. reserved for special occasions.
   d. a fact of life.

4. Proper table manners are
   a. always to be used.
   b. used only for company and at restaurants with real tablecloths.
   c. forgotten.
   d. contrived and unimportant, indicative of a superficiality of our society.

5. True/False

The tops of all canned goods should be rinsed off before the can is opened.

6. True/False

All empty cans should be rinsed out before they are recycled.

7. True/False

I like to crush aluminum cans in my hand or on my head and have walked around with them on my feet.

8. True/False

All fruits and vegetables should be rinsed and/or scrubbed before being eaten.

9. True/False

Spaghetti sauce and pizza should be meatless.

10. True/False

Whole wheat is always better.

11. True/False

Almost all foods need a little more salt or sugar or catsup.

12. How long should an unmarked container of leftovers be allowed to live in the refrigerator?

    a. for the life of the appliance

    b. until it can be submitted as a science project

    c. until it smells bad

    d. 1–3 days

    e. 1–2 weeks

    f. 1 month

13. True/False

    Etiquette should be observed when sharing a box of popcorn at a movie.

14. True/False

    No one in his or her right mind eats headless little fish out of a tin can.

15. Box cakes and premade frosting mixes

    a. are great!

    b. taste totally artificial.

    c. attest to how truly uncaring our society has become.

16. True/False

Sexual favors can be purchased from one's spouse with gourmet chocolate cookies.

17. You and your spouse have invited friends to Thanksgiving dinner. You are serving and have just scooped up some stuffing from inside the holiday bird cooked by your spouse. Unfortunately, you notice bits of paper from the unremoved giblet bag, sure signs that your beloved is about to be mortified. Several others at the table have noticed the confetti in the dressing and are waiting for your reaction.
    a. You laugh shrilly, rip the sack from its croutoned tomb, and hold a mock funeral.
    b. You deliver a sarcastic attack on your spouse's culinary abilities.
    c. You excuse yourself and take the bird into the kitchen for surgical removal of the offending bag.

18. The most elaborate dinner party I ever want to give
    a. will be black-tie, catered, with at least 75 to 150 guests.
    b. will be catered buffet-style for 10 to 25.
    c. will be a small sit-down dinner party for 8 to 10; I'll cook.
    d. will serve beer nuts and pizza and be held in honor of the Super Bowl.
    e. will be for guests under 10 years of age and catered by Ronald McDonald.

19. Paying $2.00 for a single piece of candy means you're
    a. crazy and extravagant.
    b. appreciative of fine food.
    c. going to stick a candle in it and pass it off as a birthday cake.

20. True/False
    Only women eat brunch.

21. The appropriate time for dinner is
    a. 5:30ish.
    b. 6:00 on the dot.
    c. 6:30.
    d. 7:30.
    e. 8:30.
    f. 9:30 or later.
    g. whenever we are hungry.

22. True/False
    Almost every dinner should have representatives from the four basic food groups.

23. True/False

    I believe you are what you eat.

24. True/False

    It's not important which person does most of the cooking.

25. True/False

    The person who cooks does not have to do the dishes.

26. True/False

    I like to eat with my fingers.

27. True/False

    Returning a milk container to the refrigerator with only a splash of milk in it is unacceptable.

One essay question: How do you respond to relatives, specifically spouses, licking their fingers in public? I do not mean random licking, I mean licking to remove sauce or frosting or anything that might taste good. You have thirty minutes to develop a paragraph supporting your response.

It may now be dawning on you that you are rushing toward life's banquet with a Ring-Ding-chomping, bed-crumbing, finger-licking yahoo. Remember, however, that this person is *your* yahoo and that an innocuous Dustbuster by the bed can easily dispose of those pesky little crumbs (or at least remind them the dining room's downstairs).

2 BIRTHDAY BLOWOUTS

Does your birthday fall just short of a national holiday? Do you expect people who *really* love you to fuss over you all day, giving you a beautiful cake and presents that demonstrate they began planning for the special day weeks ago? Good luck. If you are about to marry someone who is capable of giving you true "birthday gratification," your upcoming marriage has indeed been made in heaven. If your answers to the questions below indicate such satisfaction will not be forthcoming, well, the annual event isn't going to be a piece of cake.

1. When I was growing up, birthdays were
   a. a big deal—a big party, cake, presents, etc.
   b. hardly noticed (cards or small gifts).
   c. not really mentioned, thought of as unimportant.
   d. celebrated quietly with only family members.

2. On my birthday, I expect my spouse to
   a. make special plans like dinner and a nice gift.

    b. forget it because it's just another day.

    c. have a party for me and invite a lot of our friends.

3. If I don't have a birthday cake on my birthday, I will be

    a. devastated.

    b. disappointed.

    c. happy because I hate being reminded I'm a year older.

4. Gift wrapping done by department stores is

    a. a beautiful touch.

    b. an unnecessary extravagance.

    c. a necessary extravagance.

    d. a good time-saver.

5. Gifts should be opened

    a. silently, very slowly so bows and paper can be saved.

    b. ripped off, shredding wrapping mercilessly.

    c. somewhere between a and b.

6. If I receive a gift I don't like from a relative (husband, sister-in-law, mother-in-law), I will probably

     a. say I love it and keep it in a closet.

     b. say I love it and return it if I possibly can.

     c. say I love it and use it.

7. I like gifts that are
     a. personal (nighties, clothes, etc.).
     b. athletic.
     c. intellectual.
     d. expensive.
     e. handmade by my spouse.
     f. practical.

8. True/False

   I like gift certificates.

9. True/False

   I like to help pick out my own presents.

Isn't it a crying shame that even birthdays have to be held up for scrutiny? Just one day a year, can't your beloved be responsible for reading your mind and knowing what you want? Not likely.

The good news is that because your heart's desire undoubtedly *wants* to please you, he or she can be conditioned. Sobbing and howling at the end of a cakeless, candleless birthday are effective, albeit harsh, techniques. You may, thereafter, always get an annual cake but find it served somewhat sullenly by your cheerless spouse.

To avoid such unpleasantries, reconsider your communication tactics. Signing "Happy Birthday" in a foreign language a few days before the event can be a fun reminder, provided someone is listening. Plan on having a wonderful day, and if things go awry, remember, there's always next year!

3 Driving Up the Wall

Is the person behind the wheel really the one in the driver's seat? Who controls the heater, tape deck, and rear window defogger? Can unexpected squirting of windshield cleaner cause a heart attack? And, finally, who is allowed to program the radio channels? Weighty questions, yes. But ones which must be addressed now, at a time when your loved one is too enamored to tell you that you ride the brake. Once all the repair bills come to the same address and are paid from the same account, vehicular management idiosyncrasies lose their cuteness under the scrutinizing eye of your beloved codriver.

1. When a husband and wife are out for a short ride to the grocery, movie, etc., the driver should usually be
   a. the husband.
   b. the wife.
   c. whoever feels like it.

2. Putting on makeup while driving is
   a. suicidal.
   b. a fact of life.

    c. grounds for divorce.

    d. to be attempted only in an emergency.

3. Frequently exceeding the speed limit by more than 5 miles per hour is
    a. suicidal.
    b. a fact of life.
    c. grounds for divorce.
    d. to be attempted only in an emergency.

4. Strong disapproval of fellow drivers' driving habits should be shown by
    a. attempting to force them off the road.
    b. cursing and gesturing.
    c. calling the police and reporting their license plate number.
    d. keeping quiet and fuming inwardly.
    e. looking daggers at the offending oaf.
    f. just letting it go.

5. When another person is in the car, criticism of a mate's driving habits should be
    a. stifled.
    b. accelerated.

    c. used as joke material.

6. Covering objects in the car or areas of the car with simulated fur is

    a. disgusting.

    b. classy.

    c. inconceivable.

    d. allowed only for health reasons.

7. The rearview mirror is appropriate for hanging

    a. garters and panties.

    b. dice and miniature skulls.

    c. baby shoes.

    d. parking identification.

    e. nothing.

    f. nothing, but Saint Christopher is welcome on the dash.

8. A vanity mirror is

    a. a necessity.

    b. a safety hazard.

    c. narcissistic.

    d. no big deal.

9. When the two of you are having difficulty finding your destination, asking directions

    a. is the logical solution.

    b. should be done only after at least 30 minutes of aimless wandering.

    c. is a temptation never to be succumbed to.

10. Letting animals ride unrestrained in cars is

    a. a stupid idea.

    b. cute.

    c. usually unnecessary.

11. The volume of the radio or tape deck should be

    a. low.

    b. moderate.

    c. rock-concert level.

12. Talking over the sound of the radio is

    a. no big deal.

    b. irritating.

    c.   not desirable.

    d.   an invitation to be told to shut up.

13.   You're ready to buy a new car. The color of the car should be

    a.   black, dark brown, or dark blue.

    b.   red, green, or yellow.

    c.   mauve, sandalwood, or opalescent.

    d.   whatever the manufacturer has left over.

14.   The seats on your new car should be

    a.   cloth.

    b.   leather or leather simulation.

    c.   doesn't matter

15.   True/False

    Your new car must have factory air.

16.   Air conditioning in the car should be turned on only when the temperature outdoors exceeds

    a.   80°.

    b.   85°.

    c.   90°.

    d.   95°.

    e.   Never, it's bad for the environment.

17. True/False

    Mechanical car washes should be used rarely if ever, because they ruin a car's finish.

18. A newer car should be purchased

    a.   every year.

    b.   every 2–3 years.

    c.   every 4–5 years.

    d.   every 6–8 years.

    e.   only when "old Bessie" dies.

19. To the best of my recollection, I have run out of gas

    a.   never.

    b.   once or twice.

    c.   5–10 times.

    d.   more than 10 times.

20. My gas tank is always
    a. full.
    b. ½ full.
    c. ¼ full.
    d. full enough to get to my next destination (with any luck).

21. True/False
    There is no good excuse for running out of gas.

22. True/False
    I can imagine getting into an argument if my spouse let the car run out of gas.

23. Car doors should be locked
    a. at all times.
    b. at all times when no one is in the car.
    c. whenever it seems like a good idea.
    d. seldom.
    e. overnight.
    f. when I remember.
    g. never.

24.   True/False

Naming my car and treating it like a close friend is important to me.

Did turn-of-the-century couples argue about how best to ready the old horse and buggy and where to go once it and they were hitched? I suspect they did. Of course, the solution to all horse, buggy, and auto disagreements is simple: You each have your own vehicle. That way, you can just meet at the restaurant, theater, or barn dance like strangers.

Even as I suggest this idea, I know the lovebirds among you are rejecting it, intent on cooing and pecking your way down life's highway.

If you insist on riding together, think ahead. Even if your beloved swears he or she knows the exact location of the party you are to attend in fifteen minutes, look up the address. This knowledge could be what ultimately gets you to the gala (unless, of course, your sweetheart's veins pulse with true trailblazer blood, in which case the intrusion of fact may be resentfully unheeded, and you will spend the rest of the evening discovering neighborhoods you never knew existed).

Perspectives get skewed in automobiles. You may be blamed for driving too slowly if it appears the family is going to be late for its next appointment, even though your beloved was still languishing in the bath five minutes before you were to leave.

The rule for successful road travel: Let the driver drive, and switch drivers often. Or just switch off the ignition and go find a horse and buggy, or better still, walk to the barn dance.

4 No Sweat/No Regret vs. No Pain/No Gain

D o you define "exercise" as going to the kitchen during commercials to microwave some popcorn and melt butter? Or do you find the heart-pounding experience of racing for an airport gate exhilarating? When you're ill at home, would you prefer to use a bedpan rather than the bathroom if you could find somebody to empty it? Some of these questions are intrusive and crass. So, some people feel, is exercise. Woe to the marriage that attempts to blend a proud couch potato with a would-be Charles (or Charlene) Atlas. You may think that, by now, surely you know the exercise needs or non-needs of your beloved. Don't bet on it. Courtship is often a time of accommodation. After the honeymoon, thoughts previously unuttered will find their way into the open air: "How can you lie there on the couch when it's so gorgeous out?" "Are you going to watch television for another five hours tonight?" and the most dreaded comment of all, "I don't think a marathon really sounds that tough."

1. What is the earliest you have ever gotten up to do exercise of any kind?

   a. before 5 A.M.

   b. 5–7 A.M.

   c. 7–8 A.M.

    d. don't remember

    f. don't care

    g. haven't ever

2. Rate your admiration for Jack Lallane (substitute Arnold Schwarzenegger if you're under 40) on a scale from 1 to 10.

    a. Who?

    b. 1–3

    c. 3–7

    d. 7–10

3. True/False

   Club dancing is an excellent form of exercise.

4. Violent sports are good to

    a. watch.

    b. participate in.

    c. ban.

5. Running fast is

    a. the ultimate goal in life.

    b. unnecessary.

    c. unwise.

    d. only for ectomorphs.

6. Long-distance running is

    a. appropriate only for Olympic torchbearers.

    b. narcisstic.

    c. probably as damaging to the body as it is helpful.

    d. too time-consuming.

    e. excellent discipline for mind and body.

7. True/False

Tennis, golf, and racquetball can become addictions.

8. True/False

Most worthwhile exercise needs special shoes or equipment.

9. Equipment and clothing for exercise should cost

    a. under $50.

    b. under $100.

    c. under $1,000.

    d. no limit

10. I would prefer to exercise

    a. alone.

    b. with friends.

    c. with strangers.

    d. with a candy bar or milk shake.

    e. not at all.

11. I like to learn new athletic skills

    a. by myself.

    b. from a qualified instructor.

    c. with a friend.

    d. from a friend.

    e. in a group of strangers.

    f. only if they relate to sex.

12. A good workout lasts

    a. as long as I can stand it.

    b. 15–30 minutes.

    c. under an hour.

    d. 1–2 hours.

    e. 2–4 hours.

    f. more than 4 hours.

13. I *should* work out

    a. once a week.

    b. every day.

    c. 2–3 times a week.

    d. never if I don't feel like it.

14. When you are exercising, pain

    a. means stop.

    b. is a challenge to work through.

    c. varies and should be reacted to appropriately.

15. Being in good shape means

    a. being able to bench-press your own weight or better.

    b. no flab.

    c. having a lot of energy and overall sense of perkiness.

    d. being able to walk up one or two flights of stairs without gasping and holding your side.

My fond hope at this juncture is that you couch potatoes are racing to the bedroom to de-dust-bunny those running shoes buried in the back of your closet. Their purchase inspired by the Olympics, they normally surface once every four years during the Summer Games.

To think they are going to be dragged early into the light of day is thrilling. (The fact that their newness is spattered with Gatorade stains from novices unable to run and chug at the same time is irrelevant.)

Others of you are not running anywhere and are not about to. You are staring numbly into space. This quiz has confirmed your worst suspicions: You are about to marry a true exercise zealot, the Radical Runner. Snow, rain, and sleet are scorned by R.R.'s sodden feet. This individual welcomes the challenge of running through pulled hamstrings and strained relationships. When nature calls, the Radical Runner simply detours behind a bush.

Whether you are couch potatoes or Radical Runners, another type of workout is even more important to your health than physical exercise. Skip bench-pressing triple your own weight and try, when you least want to, holding your tongue.

5 You Wouldn't Like Me When I'm Angry

Irritated. Miffed. Seriously ticked off. How is one's mate to read the beloved's emotional barometer? After all, one person's deadly silence is another's peace and quiet. Consider all the nuances of body language and speech pattern that must be skillfully interpreted when your spouse is feeling adversarial. If you are so unfortunate as to misread these signs, tiny little disagreements can blow into raging power struggles. Have you ever engaged in a raging power struggle? Trust me, the niceties of confrontational sparring observed during courtship wither, leaving both of you exposed and ill prepared for your First Married Fight.

1. Fighting is
    a. good because it clears the air.
    b. bad because wounds inflicted can be slow to heal.
    c. a normal part of marriage.
    d. to be avoided at almost all costs.

2. My parents argued
    a. a lot.

    b. rarely.

    c. occasionally.

3. When my parents argued, I
- a. left the house.
- b. chose sides and jumped in.
- c. listened and got upset.
- d. tuned them out.

4. When I get angry, the main thing I do is
- a. cry.
- b. yell.
- c. sulk.
- d. swear.
- e. throw things.
- f. get sarcastic.

5. When I get mad at things or people other than you, I need you to
- a. ask me questions to draw the problem out of me.
- b. listen to me blow off steam and not say much.

    c. offer advice, solicited or otherwise.

    d. always take my side.

    e. hug me.

6. When I get mad at you, I want you to

    a. leave me alone to work it out myself.

    b. get mad at me too.

    c. be rational and not react.

    d. hug me.

7. When I say "Nothing's wrong," I mean it

    a. 100 percent of the time.

    b. 75 percent of the time.

    c. 50 percent of the time.

    d. 25 percent of the time.

    e. 0 percent of the time.

8. When I say "Just leave me alone," I mean it

    a. 100 percent of the time.

    b. 75 percent of the time.

    c. 50 percent of the time.

    d. 25 percent of the time.

    e. 0 percent of the time.

9. Throwing things is a legitimate expression of anger.

    a. never

    b. at home

    c. anywhere

10. Making a scene in public is

    a. inexcusable.

    b. sometimes justifiable.

    c. a perfectly normal expression of discontent.

11. True/False

    I hold grudges.

Anger produces arguments, correct? Certainly not. Sometimes it just produces divorces without the unpleasant preliminaries. Knowing this fact, I am compelled to help you handle this potentially destructive emotion and to see its brighter side.

- *Don't* pretend you are not angry when you are.
- *Don't* ignore your feelings, hoping they will dissolve in a few days. This attitude promotes the "curse causeless" syndrome, which manifests itself as a rage over an insignificant remark three days after the original hurt.
- *Don't* introduce old issues or victories to bolster your position.
- *Don't* use sarcasm.
- *Don't* hit.
- *Do* say specifically what is making you angry. Be prepared to work with your beloved to recognize your fury's true source.
- *Do* try to see another side to the remark or situation serving as catalyst to your ire.
- *Do* remember the person you want to scream at loves you and doesn't usually want to see you upset and hurting.
- *Do* remember, before you wade into battle, the last sweet thing your love has said or done.

6 Kitties, Puppies, and Pythons

Fluff. Sparky. Xerxes. Edith. All wonderful, furry companions are occasional royal pains. Now is the time to level about your allergy to cat hair or your dislike of miniature anythings that hop and yip like windup toys. Remember, too, a fondness for man's best friend can be diminished by a spouse who always hands you the pooper-scooper.

1. Pets should have names like
   a. Spot, Tippy, Red Dog, Fluff.
   b. Igor, Francois, Freud.
   c. Fred, Mary, Al.
   d. Hey Mutt, Damn Cat.

2. Cat boxes should be cleaned
   a. every day.
   b. every other day.
   c. once a week.
   d. when the cat starts defecating on the laundry.

3. True/False
   Cats should be indoor animals.

4. People who have cats' claws removed are
   a. selfish and egocentric.
   b. practical.

5. The only kind of dog I would have is
   a. a large dog—collie, German shepherd.
   b. a stray.
   c. a pedigree.
   d. a poodle, cockapoo, or shih tzu.
   e. a stuffed one.

6. True/False
   Pets make excellent status symbols.

7. The care of the pet is the responsibility of
   a. the person who wanted it.
   b. mutual.

c. the first person available for the specific need.

d. the one the animal likes best.

8. True/False

Pets are wonderful traveling companions.

9. You are moving across the country. Your dog of three years will be

a. given away.

b. traveling in the car with you.

c. sedated and shipped by air.

d. sent to the Humane Society.

e. put to sleep.

f. left in the street.

10. Dogs were meant to

a. live on farms.

b. be chained or penned in a yard.

c. be in the house almost all the time.

d. run the neighborhood.

11. True/False
    When the weather justifies it, pets should be dressed like people.

12. True/False
    All responsible pet owners neuter their pets.

13. Your beloved Fido is 9 years old and needs major surgery to the tune of $300. You
    a. order the vet to put him to sleep.
    b. take a second job if necessary to afford the operation.
    c. wait awhile to see if he gets better by himself.

14. Pets should eat
    a. at the table.
    b. in the basement.
    c. outside.
    d. in the kitchen on the floor.

15. Dry pet food is
    a. economical and nutritious.
    b. cruel and unusual punishment.
    c. okay if it's supplemented with canned food or table scraps.

16. True/False

    A begging dog is a cute dog.

17. True/False

    Kennels are acceptable places to keep animals while owners are out of town.

18. Pets should do tricks only if
    a. they really want to.
    b. they can make money at it.
    c. their owners are disrespectful, easily amused boobs.
    d. it makes people laugh.

19. Pets should be punished by
    a. isolating them.
    b. hitting them with newspapers.
    c. throwing them down the stairs.
    d. shaking your finger at them, saying, "Naughty, naughty baby."

20. True/False

    A desirable pet enjoys killing its dinner.

What about a Chia pet? True, it is possible that your "real" pet will eat your Chia, but Chia ownership advantages still outweigh the risk. Defining which is your "real" pet, when both grow, need nourishment, and provide hours of companionship is a philosophical exercise we will not indulge in at this time.

Let us, instead, get to the heart of pet ownership and its motivation. A friend's Afghan hounds looked quite elegant when he proudly paraded them up and down the street outside his efficiency apartment. However, when they paraded themselves around inside the apartment, they neither looked elegant nor smelled it. Ditto for the apartment.

Perhaps basing our self-image on the acquisition of feline, canine, or porcine comrades is not wise if the pets' living conditions will cause their own self-esteem and sense of self-worth to plummet.

Another question you might ask yourselves: What actions represent an unacceptable level of violence when disciplining a pet? I have seen a mischievous kitten become suddenly airborne when he playfully teethed on my intended's arm. My beloved "just gave him a little push." I called that cruel and unusual punishment—he called it survival.

7 BATHROOM ETIQUETTE: THE TOILET SEAT DILEMMA

Have you ever had your very own *private* bathroom? Trivial question, right? Surely love can overcome the Colgate-versus-Gleem conflict. But can love conquer the repulsion you feel at your beloved's flossing fallout on the bathroom mirror each morning? Will you really be able to overlook the fact that your striking reflection at sunrise is flecked with last night's corn on the cob? Let's be honest. Lurking among the pristine porcelain and shining tiles are marital land mines. Deceptively hygienic looking, the bathroom can become a battlefield where everybody fights dirty.

1. The length of my average shower is
   a. about 10 minutes.
   b. about 20 minutes.
   c. about 30 minutes.
   d. longer than 30 minutes.

2. True/False
   A lot of water is wasted by long showers.

3. True/False

   Bars of soap should not be transferred from the shower/tub to the sink and vice versa except in emergencies.

4. True/False

   The walls of a glassed shower should be dried by the showeree immediately after he or she turns off the water.

5. The person who should clean the tub/shower is
   a. the week's designated cleaner.
   b. the husband.
   c. the wife.
   d. whoever thinks it's dirty.

6. Hair in the tub or sink should be
   a. forced down the drain immediately.
   b. left to accumulate until the drain is completely clogged.
   c. cleaned up by the person missing the most hair.

7. True/False

To keep the bathroom floor as dry as possible, one should dry off inside the tub or shower.

8. Use of a bath mat is
   a. important.
   b. unimportant.
   c. a hassle.

9. The proper place for a bath towel you have just used for the first time is
   a. the dirty-clothes hamper.
   b. the doorknob.
   c. the floor.
   d. the bed.
   e. the towel rack.

10. When a towel is dirty, you
    a. throw it down the chute or put it in the clothes hamper.
    b. hang it up to dry, then throw it in the hamper.
    c. do a load of laundry.
    d. hang it up and leave it there because you can't decide if it's really dirty.

    e. throw it on the floor or bed.

11. You discover your spouse uses your toothbrush when his/hers has been misplaced.

    a. You don't care—you've swapped spit before.

    b. You say nothing but buy a new toothbrush for yourself.

    c. You tell your spouse just how gross and disgusting you think toothbrush borrowing is.

    d. You use your spouse's toothbrush to see how he or she likes it.

12. Globs of toothpaste in the sink are the responsibility of

    a. the spitter.

    b. the one who is offended.

    c. the maid.

    d. no one—they will go away by themselves.

13. True/False

Flossing is unnecessary and a hassle.

14. True/False

A person should never floss while looking in the mirror.

15. The drinking glass in the bathroom should
    a. be plastic.
    b. match the decor.
    c. be digital—nothing more than my hand.
    d. be disposable.
    e. Who cares?

16. True/False
    The sink and surrounding area should be dried after each use.

17. Shampoos, conditioners, etc., should be kept
    a. on the edge of the tub.
    b. in a bath caddy.
    c. in a medicine cabinet or somewhere else out of sight.

18. True/False
    When you're taking a shower, the bathroom door should be left open a little so steam doesn't fog the mirror.

19. The proper position for a toilet seat is
    a. cover down.

    b. cover up, seat down.

    c. cover up, seat up.

20. Special hand towels and decorative soaps are needed

    a. never.

    b. when the Queen of England visits.

    c. only for special company.

    d. every day.

21. Bubble baths are:

    a. a waste of money.

    b. bad for your skin.

    c. whimsical and relaxing.

    d. a personal matter.

22. Locking the bathroom door is

    a. vital.

    b. rude.

    c. optional.

23. Ideally, bathroom floors should be
    a. tiled.
    b. hardwood.
    c. carpeted.

24. People who do other tasks that require water while you are in the shower should be
    a. screamed at for their thoughtlessness, no expletives deleted.
    b. requested to try to remember when the shower is in use.
    c. treated as if nothing happened—it's not worth an argument.

25. True/False
    I like to read in the bathroom.

26. True/False
    I have had the exciting experience of falling into a seat-up toilet at 3 A.M.

27. True/False
    Shelves in the medicine cabinet should be assigned.

Hours after taking my own vows, I committed the rarely forgiven sin of leaving the cap off the toothpaste. Apparently, this is the cosmic sign of related character flaws such as toilet-paper-wasting and bathroom hogging. Cognizant of this disturbing fact, my new husband chastised me soundly.

Because we frequent the powder room so regularly, we must agree on its appearance, cleaning, and use. Those of you wondering why "use" is included probably plan to use the bathroom as a giant clothes hamper or as an extension of your library.

A few recommendations: (1) Don't laugh at the color or texture of your beloved's choice of toilet paper. (I know colored t.p. is bad for the environment, but it's good for the decorating scheme, so broach this issue gently.) (2) Don't laugh at the color or texture of your partner's toothbrush. If your beloved likes hard bristles and you know dentists recommend soft, before you share this knowledge, remember, these are not your teeth!

8 HEAT AND LIGHTS

Most people mistakenly believe the world's most powerful person can, with one touch of a button, blast us all into nuclear oblivion. In actuality, true power rests with the individual who can, with the twirl of a dial, reduce the temperature in a home to fifty degrees and then cheerfully say, "Good night, honey." Yes, as you suspected, the supreme power over all happiness and health resides with the Controller of the Thermostat. Very simply put, if during your marriage, you will be said Controller, you will be happy. If you generously, but unwisely, attempt to share the control, you and your beloved will bicker endlessly about the thinness of the other's skin and blood or the thickness of the other's skull. To mix metaphors, some like it hot, some like it cold, and never the twain shall meet.

A thousand points of light. Porch lights glowing with neighborliness and hospitality. Or are they, instead, blatant advertisements of a spendthrift nature? Those who have enjoyed leaving lights on since childhood, find it difficult to put a price tag on the warm, homey, secure feeling lots of lights ablazing give. Others less friendly (or less neurotic, depending on your perspective) regard lights left on—in the bathroom, in the hallway, in the kitchen, etc.—as a sinful waste of electricity and money. Incidentally, my

limited research has shown that light turner-offers are usually also temperature drop-
pers. Go figure.

1. At bedtime the thermostat should be
    a. set at 70° or above.
    b. set at around 65°.
    c. set at around 60°.
    d. set at 55°.
    e. turned off.

2. In cold weather, if people are home during the day, the thermostat should be set
    at
    a. 75° or above.
    b. 70°.
    c. 65° or below.

3. In cold weather, if no one is home, the thermostat should be
    a. set at 75° or higher.
    b. set at 70°.
    c. set at 65° or lower.

d. turned off.

4. True/False

If people are cold, instead of turning up the heat, they should put on more clothes.

5. True/False

Using lots of blankets on the bed is better than turning up the heat.

6. True/False

I like to sleep with the window open a little bit no matter what the season.

7. Space heaters are

a. practical.

b. too expensive to use.

c. unnecessary.

d. a fire hazard.

8. True/False

People who bundle up in two sweaters, three pairs of socks, and gloves to try to stay warm in a cold house really bother me.

9. True/False

   People who keep their house at 80 degrees in the winter and dress like it's summer really bother me.

10. True/False

    Spouses should wear nothing or next to it in bed, no matter what the season or temperature.

11. For me, staying warm in cold weather is

    a. a frequent problem.

    b. an occasional problem.

    c. no problem at all.

12. For me, staying cool in the summer is

    a. rarely a problem.

    b. sometimes a problem.

    c. often a problem.

13. If I had to feel one or the other, I'd rather be a little

    a. too cool.

    b. too warm.

14. If I'm physically uncomfortable, I'll
    a. whine a lot.
    b. try to fix the problem.
    c. grin and bear it.
    d. keep still for the moment and complain later.

15. Electric blankets are
    a. not to be used because they can fry you while you sleep.
    b. great.
    c. unnecessary.
    d. not comfortable or desirable.

16. Air conditioning is
    a. dangerous to your health.
    b. too expensive to use very much.
    c. dangerous to the environment.
    d. addictive.

17. Air conditioning is an absolute necessity when the temperature outside hits
    a. 80°.

    b. 85°.

    c. 90°.

    d. 95°.

    e. It's never a necessity.

18. Night-lights for adults are
    a. signs of cowardice.
    b. signs of the way to the bathroom.
    c. signs of security and reassurance.
    d. extravagant.
    e. unnecessary.

19. Porch lights should be on
    a. all night, every night.
    b. until bedtime.
    c. when company arrives and departs.
    d. never.
    e. until someone remembers to turn them off.

20. Back porch lights should be turned on
    a. at dusk each evening.
    b. when an intruder is suspected.
    c. for late arrivals.
    d. never.

21. Lights in a room should be turned off when one
    a. doesn't intend to reenter the room soon (within 10 minutes).
    b. leaves the room.
    c. leaves the dwelling.
    d. wants to.

22. True/False
    Dim lights (75 watts and under) are depressing when used as the only light in the living room, kitchen, bathroom, etc.

23. True/False
    Buying 5-year bulbs is a stupid idea.

24. True/False

Seeing less than a full complement of bulbs in a fixture (chandelier, etc.) is
depressing.

The path to the thermostat in my childhood home was well trodden. It was not a
path my mother or father trod silently. Many a winter's eve my father complained that
while he was out earning our daily bread, we, with malice aforethought, turned the
thermostat to ninety. Apparently, he envisioned us romping through the house, mid-
January, mid-Nebraska, clad only in shorts and halter tops, as he tramped through the
snow. None of my mother's protestations could convince him otherwise. Only a study
of the thermostat could reassure him we were not playing beach blanket bingo with his
hard-earned cash.

Similarly, at night Mother was certain Father, intent on revenge, set the thermostat much below the agreed-upon temperature of sixty-five.

I don't know if Mother and Father wearied of their frequent temperature control
tiffs, but as a child, I certainly did. I suggest you establish reasonable guidelines and
honor them. It's amazing how little arguments, over time, can chill and darken a home.
And then, trust me, warming up is much harder than just turning a dial.

9 "I'm on Fire!" and Other Revealing Kitchen Quotes

Do you cook? I mean in the kitchen, using proper measuring utensils, designer cookbooks, and impressive vocabulary? (Do you really know what "roux" means?) A distinction must be made at this point. The following questions will relate not to meal content, but rather to the intricacies of meal preparation—your inclination toward exploding forgotten potatoes in a hot oven or accidentally chocolate-coating a space heater with once-frozen chocolate chips. Time to shoo all those ghosts out of your culinary closet and confess that not *one* of your pots or pans is suitable for hanging and that, from the looks of your skillets, you've probably ingested Teflon.

1. True/False

   I swear I have never melted a plastic hot-dog-bun bag to the side of the toaster, causing the toaster to read "Wonder Buns" in red, white, and blue.

2. Mistaking the 1-cup measure for the ½-cup measure and consequently producing leaden cookies is

   a. the act of an idiot.

    b. a natural mistake to be giggled over and forgotten.

    c. never to be revealed to anyone; chuck the whole batch.

    d. an act which will, justifiably, hold you up for ridicule for many years to come.

3. Preheating an oven is

    a. the first step to baking success.

    b. unnecessary.

    c. something that's good to do if you have time.

4. True/False

    I must begin with a completely clean kitchen.

5. People who *must* clean up after every step of food and meal preparation are

    a. wise and orderly.

    b. neurotic.

    c. unknown to me.

6. If you step into the kitchen as I'm preparing a meal and start asking questions or giving advice, I will probably

    a. try to be polite but not appreciate the distraction.

    b. follow your suggestions if they're good.

    c. tell you to shut up or do it yourself.

    d. get nervous, lose my place in the recipe book, and start burning things.

7. How many components of a meal must be burned before it's considered to be a failure?

    a. 1

    b. 2

    c. 3–4

    d. Nothing has to be burned to make a meal a failure.

8. True/False

I have personally seen food explode.

9. True/False

I have personally been responsible for food exploding.

10. True/False

I have on at least one occasion mistaken sugar for salt or vice versa.

11. True/False

One of my fondest childhood memories is licking the cake batter off Mom's wooden spoon and beaters.

12. Whipping cream must be
    a. beaten carefully in a deep bowl or with an appropriate cover to avoid splattering.
    b. beaten real fast.
    c. artificial.
    d. squirted from an aerosol can so it can taste like fluorocarbons.

13. True/False
    I have one or more times beaten whipping cream into butter.

14. True/False
    I know how to separate eggs (yolks from whites).

15. True/False
    I own or want to own an omelette pan.

16. True/False
    I own or want to own a waffle iron.

17. I have made cakes from scratch and must say
    a. I enjoyed doing so very much.

b. they were inedible.

c. they were misshapen and grotesque and made presentable only by four cans of frosting.

18. True/False

I know the difference between frosting and icing.

19. Potato salad must contain

a. eggs.

b. bacon.

c. mustard.

d. onions.

e. all of the above.

20. True/False

I love to marinate.

21. True/False

Barbecueing is an art.

22. When I barbecue, my mood is usually

    a. festive.

    b. morose.

    c. reflective.

    d. hostile.

23. True/False

To look palatable, carrot sticks and celery sticks must be cut and arranged uniformly.

24. True/False

I enjoy mutilating sheet cakes and transforming them into barking dogs and space shuttles.

25. True/False

Flower petals and other decorative vegetation on one's plate enhance dining pleasure.

26. True/False

Almost any meal had in a restaurant could have been prepared at home with relative ease.

27. The best way to put out a small grease fire on the stove is to
   a. call the fire department.
   b. put a lid on it.
   c. douse it with baking soda.
   d. use the fire extinguisher.

28. True/False
   I rarely sift.

29. True/False
   I enjoy boning.

30. True/False
   I will not allow pets on the counter when I cook.

   "The way to a man's heart is through his stomach." Hmmm. I am not certain that expression still holds true. However, I am confident of the validity of its variation: "The way to a nervous breakdown is to expect yourself to prepare three delicious, nutritious meals every day for the rest of your life."

   I should not make that assumption. Many people express their love by browning, broiling, and baking up a storm, much to the delight of their loved ones. Maybe it is a matter of expectations. May I suggest you take a few moments to review yours. Talk about how many times a week you expect to go to a restaurant or get carryout. Talk about who is going to pay.

Also discuss how often you expect to invite others to your home to share the joys of your cooking. If you haven't much food preparation experience, you may want to resist asking unsuspecting acquaintances with high hopes and empty tummies to sample one of your untested concoctions. I speak from personal experience.

Twenty-two and married only four months, I was unschooled in the culinary arts. In my ignorance, I foolishly welcomed my husband's suggestion to invite a fellow army draftee to dinner. Actually, it was to be a bit more than that. It was to be Guest Dave's last meal before being shipped to the war zone.

Wanting to make the somber occasion somewhat festive, I planned a dining extravaganza using my new recipes for fruit ambrosia, mostaccioli, and chicken parmesan.

And what an event it was. Guest Dave appeared at our door looking a little depressed, having just put his pregnant wife on the plane for her mother's. Little did Dave know that that farewell would be the high point of his day.

After the introductions, I graciously glided toward the table, the men following, bewitched I'm sure. Guest Dave, now seated, commented on the beauty of the table and picked up his napkin. Then he screamed. All right, perhaps it wasn't an actual scream, but it was certainly more than getting stuck by that little price tag pin on the napkin warranted. A Band-Aid was not supposed to be part of the first course.

Having apologized profusely and seeing that the flow of blood had ebbed if not stopped, I gave him another pink napkin from my wedding present collection. This is the unfortunate part. Because my delicate hostess sensibilities had become unbalanced, I did not remove the price tag or its offending pin from the second napkin either. Déjà vu.

We continued the meal in silence, Guest Dave handling his fork somewhat awkwardly at this point. He did, however, manage to get a bite of mostaccioli into his mouth. (It is important to mention here, in my defense, that Dave had been less than punctual; the pasta had waited patiently in its water for him for some time. Sauce was added just before serving.)

To continue with Dave, the Wounded and the Starving. I must admit, I watched him surreptitiously, expecting accolades after he finished his first bite of my first company dinner.

Unfortunately, Dave was not destined to swallow that first morsel. I watched in horror as he stopped chewing and began gesticulating, face flushed and eyes bulging. In a macabre pantomime, he pointed alternately at his mouth, which he could not seem to open, and at his water glass. I thrust the glass into his hands, and he somehow forced his lips apart and threw the water at his face. With that lubricant, he could gaspingly expel into his napkin the swollen mostaccioli responsible for gluing his tongue to the roof of his mouth and suffocating him.

After this heart-stopping dinner, we adjourned to a small card table in the living room for an evening of merriment. Make that ten minutes. After Guest Dave hurt his tooth on my mismeasured oatmeal cookies (see question 2), he left abruptly, muttering something that sounded like "Bring on the rice."

To his credit and my relief, my husband never said an unkind word about the disastrous evening.

Many lessons can be learned from this experience: Use paper napkins, remove pasta quickly from water after cooking, and invite guests with a sense of humor.

10   Leaving on a Jet Plane: Do You Hate to Go?

Nights in Zanzibar; a language impossible to understand spoken by exotic natives who write backward; the sun's meltdown over a breathtaking mountain range whose name you can't pronounce. These experiences are worth a lot, wouldn't you agree? They give our lives texture, dimension, and perspective and allow us to appreciate foreign cultures. Or these experiences give us anxiety attacks, homesickness, Montezuma's revenge, empty bank accounts, and absolute lust to eat a Big Mac, fries, and a chocolate shake.

1. True/False

   I have accidentally locked my keys in the trunk of the car to postpone taking a long road trip.

2. A "spontaneous" trip means planning was done

   a. no more than 30 minutes before departure.

   b. no more than 8 hours before departure.

   c. at least 2 weeks in advance.

   d. at least 2 months in advance.

3. My idea of a faraway place is
   a. the Hindu Kush.
   b. Istanbul.
   c. London.
   d. Ohio.

4. Traveling first class is
   a. an unjustifiable extravagance.
   b. a justifiable extravagance.
   c. the only way to go.
   d. unknown in my experience.

5. When I fly, I just want the plane
   a. to have the president of McDonnell-Douglas or Boeing on it.
   b. to be large and have many engines.
   c. *not* to have a cute puddle-jumper name like Sunset Air.
   d. to stay on the ground indefinitely so I have to find another mode of transportation.
   e. to have a pilot.

6. When I travel by plane, I dress
   a. to impress.
   b. for the occasion—suits for business, leis for Maui.
   c. casually.
   d. like a slob.

7. True/False
   Airlines frequently lose my baggage.

8. True/False
   I have never missed a flight.

9. To me, getting to the airport or train station "early" means
   a. the plane or train hasn't left yet.
   b. a half hour before departure
   c. at least 1 hour before departure.

10. True/False
    I don't mind paying $4.50 for a hot dog at an airport.

11. True/False

     My luggage has wheels.

12. The need to sit on a suitcase to close it shows

     a. poor packing technique.

     b. impatience and ill humor.

     c. decisive emergency action.

13. True/False

     Women can and should carry heavy suitcases in the presence of able-bodied, empty-handed males.

14. Traveling all day (7 A.M.–7 P.M.) by car requires a certain number of rest stops:

     a. 2.

     b. 3–4.

     c. 5–6.

     d. unlimited, unscheduled, spontaneous.

15. On road trips, food should be

     a. carried in large quantities from home.

     b. purchased at local grocery stores.

    c. enjoyed at restaurants.

    d. combinations of above.

16. My idea of "roughing it" means

    a. taking a tent, K rations, and a flashlight into the jungle, forest, swamp, or mountains or my choice.

    b. using an RV to explore America.

    c. going to a Marriott or Hilton and ordering room service.

17. A good length for a vacation is

    a. 3 days.

    b. 1–2 weeks.

    c. 3–5 weeks.

    d. 2–3 months.

18. True/False

Spouses should never or rarely take vacations separately.

19. On my vacation I want to see

    a. a deer.

    b. a mountain.

     c. a golf course.

     d. no people.

     e. a fish.

     f. a room service menu.

     g. a play or concert.

     h. a heart-shaped bed.

     i. Las Vegas showgirls.

     j. One of the Seven Wonders.

20. As far as spending money on a vacation goes, I believe

     a. going as economically as possible is the only practical thing to do.

     b. blowing a wad is necessary to having a good time.

     c. very little money needs to be spent to have an enjoyable time.

21. A reasonable time to start driving each day is

     a. before 5:30 A.M.

     b. 5:30–7:30 A.M.

     c. about 8 or 9 A.M.

     d. 10 A.M.

22. A reasonable time to stop traveling is
    a. 5–6 P.M.
    b. 6–8 P.M.
    c. 8–10 P.M.
    d. 10 P.M.–midnight.
    e. whenever you're tired.

23. True/False

    Driving all night is usually the fastest, most practical way to get anywhere.

24. True/False

    I enjoy driving late at night.

25. Reservations
    a. should be made well in advance and double-checked to confirm.
    b. are usually restrictive and unnecessary and spoil the spontaneity of the trip.
    c. can be made the day of or day prior to departure.

26. True/False

    Pets make good traveling companions.

27. True/False

Someday I would like to take a shuttle to the moon.

28. Trips should be taken

   a. once a month.

   b. once a year.

   c. once a lifetime.

   d. whenever we feel like it.

   e. whenever we can afford it.

After the back seat of the car had been removed, my sensitive toes explored the trunk and found the keys Husband had accidentally locked in it. At that moment, over my protestations, the gas station attendant bludgeoned the lock one last time, shattering it to the cheers of Husband and three "mechanics."

This incident took place one mile from our home as we—Husband, Wife, Child, and Lhasa Apso—began a three-hour holiday sojourn to a cabana on the ocean. After some reflection, Husband opined that, because there are no "accidents," he must have been demonstrating his dislike of family vacations by locking the car keys in the trunk.

Golly, golly, golly. Wouldn't it have been easier to say "Gosh, honey, why don't you take the whining kid and the yipping, barfing dog to the shore for Thanksgiving and blow that seven hundred bucks yourself?" Oh well, 20/20 hindsight.

In your case, we are talking about foresight. Do you and your beloved want to travel for the same reasons? Do you want to travel at all? Mandatory fun has such a wearying ring to it. Creative compromise before and during the trip means a good time should be had by all; nevertheless, carry your own keys.

11 SEX

Marriage means plumbing the depths of erotic experience and enjoyment. It means night after sweaty night of sensual exploration and adventure. Time will only heighten your appreciation of your partner's sexuality and prowess. Do you believe this? Don't. For a lot of people, the above statements are false after the first year of wedded bliss. But no matter, you reply, you are not so base as to place so much importance on such a carnal act. Don't hand me that. (A personal note: If you have a history of sexual activity but you are weary of it and plan to marry "just a good friend," give the ring back immediately.)

1. True/False
    I will never question my spouse about previous sexual experiences.

2. In all honesty, I would prefer my betrothed to be
    a. a virgin.
    b. somewhat experienced.
    c. very experienced.
    d. deflowered before marriage by me.

3. During the first year of marriage, I imagine we'll have sex
   a. daily (at least once).
   b. 3–5 times a week.
   c. weekly.
   d. once every 3 or 4 weeks.

4. To me the most meaningful part of sex is
   a. foreplay.
   b. orgasm.
   c. afterglow.
   d. all of the above.

5. Foreplay should last
   a. What's foreplay?
   b. about 2–5 minutes.
   c. 15–30 minutes.
   d. 30–60 minutes.
   e. I don't time these things; it depends on the situation.
   f. more than an hour.

6. True/False

   Every satisfying sexual experience must culminate in orgasm.

7. Faking orgasm is
   a. unthinkable.
   b. deceptive and unacceptable.
   c. an act of compassion.
   d. an occasional "easy out."

8. True/False

   I expect a lot of sexual experimentation to be part of our marriage.

9. Vasectomy as a birth control measure is
   a. a possibility.
   b. a probability.
   c. doubtful.
   d. an impossibility.

10. True/False

    Fruits and vegetables are appropriate sexual aids.

11. Flavored oils and edible underwear are

   a. obvious signs of a decadent society.

   b. too kinky for me.

   c. great!

   d. great! (probably)

12. True/False

   Sex is for the bedroom, on the bed, only.

13. True/False

   Birth control is primarily the woman's responsibility.

Does the subject of sex embarrass you? Are you too embarrassed to say "yes"? Better to blush slightly now than to become seriously cranky later. Actually, "cranky" may not be the right word. Then again, it may not be the wrong word if, night after night, you feel you are getting the short end of the stick, so to speak.

As a young bride, a wedding night defloweree, my desire to be alluring to my husband emboldened me. One evening my negligee and I floated into the living room, where my husband was reading the paper. I rubbed seductively against his arm, murmuring something about the editorials, I think. He responded tersely, "Don't you know men make the advances; when I want it, I'll let you know."

If you imagine I felt embarrassed, ashamed, rejected, confused, and ultimately undesirable, you are very perceptive. I share this humiliating little slice of life with you to suggest how closely vulnerability and the bedroom are tied. It is, I believe, where our feelings can be most quickly and most deeply hurt, whether we are inclined to admit it or not.

One final note: Those of you who enjoy fantasizing and regard it as a natural part of marriage might want to confirm that your spouse-to-be feels the same. Strange how few spouses who enjoyed chatting with the bank teller at noon appreciate being told in the heat of midnight passion that their beloved's vivid imagination has transported said teller to the marital bed to inspire a truly galactic conjugal experience.

12 OH, I GUESS I FORGOT TO TELL YOU
I WROTE THAT CHECK

Penny, nickel, dime. Small change. If you drop one in the street or in the car and don't pick it up, it doesn't matter. Buy a soda, mostly ice, for eighty-nine cents—no big deal. Don't feel like eating everything on your plate? No problem. What's this? A fly in the financial ointment? You say you are marrying an individual who lives by the credos "A penny saved is a penny earned," "Waste not, want not," "Find a penny, pick it up . . ."? Your honey loves brown-bagging it and thermoses of homemade soup? To your future mate, extravagance is paying full price for a pizza instead of waiting until 11 P.M. to get the ones for half price that nobody's picked up.

If both of you appreciate the value of a dollar or are stingy tightwads, depending on one's perspective, you will hurdle with ease one of marriage's greatest obstacles: money management. If both of you agree money is made to be spent and feel conspicuous consumption is delightfully all-American, you too will be happy if in fact you can make truckloads of bucks. However, very few housemates share identical views on money—the making of it, the spending of it, the saving of it. And, let's be honest, who wants to argue about something as unromantic and crass as money before the wedding. This is unfortunate, because during your marital lifetimes, about 50 percent of your conversations and about 75 percent of all of your fights will be about money and you will have had *no practice.*

1. Paper plates and cups
    a. should be used at picnics only.
    b. can supplement regular dinnerware.
    c. should be used daily—why spend a lot of money on dishes you have to wash?
    d. are a waste of money and trees.
    e. are for lazy and extravagant people.

2. Going out to eat at nice restaurants is
    a. for special occasions only.
    b. a nice date for the weekend.
    c. the way I fix dinner several nights a week.

3. True/False
    I like escargot and caviar.

4. True/False
    I am usually close to my limit on my credit cards.

5. True/False

   I have been denied credit.

6. When I near the top of my credit limit on a card, I
   a. feel pressured and nervous.
   b. get depressed.
   c. ask for a higher limit.
   d. don't care at all.
   e. stop using the card completely to get the balance down.

7. True/False

   I think having credit cards is a bad idea.

8. True/False

   I prefer living in a house to living in an apartment.

9. I think frequent impulse buying is
   a. cute.
   b. unjustified and wasteful.
   c. sometimes a good idea.

10. Money should be

    a. spent on a lot of neat material stuff.

    b. spent on bare necessities of life—the rest should be saved.

    c. spent on experiences like travel, theater, etc.

    d. given to helping those less fortunate.

11. I think most loans (not car or house) and credit cards have an interest rate of

    a. 5 percent.

    b. 10 percent.

    c. 15 percent.

    d. 20 percent.

    e. 25 percent.

12. If we choose, we should be able to buy a home

    a. immediately.

    b. within 1–2 years.

    c. within 2–5 years.

    d. within 5–10 years.

13. You have a perfectly good jacket, but L.L. Bean has a perfectly better one you really want to order. You will probably
    a. order it immediately if you've got the money.
    b. order it immediately and figure you can get the money before the check hits the bank.
    c. hint to relatives that you want it for Christmas, birthday, etc.
    d. save for it.

14. True/False

    I get more pleasure buying for others than I do for myself.

15. I buy designer labels
    a. never or rarely.
    b. 10–20 percent of the time.
    c. 20–40 percent of the time.
    d. 40–60 percent of the time.
    e. 60–80 percent of the time.
    f. 80–100 percent of the time.

16. Garage sales
    a. depress me.

    b. thrill me.

    c. are unknown to me.

    d. are mildly interesting to me.

17. The final decision on major purchases should be made

    a. jointly.

    b. by the person who makes the most money.

    c. by the person who has researched the product.

18. True/False

I have received a large sum of money through an insurance settlement, inheritance, lottery, etc.

19. True/False

I think gambling is fun and a good way to make money.

20. True/False

Sometimes I like to spend money when I'm depressed.

21. True/False

I always pay my bills right on time.

22. When I say I'm out of money, I mean
    a. I don't have any cash on me; I need to get some from the bank.
    b. my cash and checking account are depleted.
    c. my cash and checking and savings accounts are depleted.
    d. my cash and checking and savings accounts are depleted, and I've sold the stocks and real estate—like I said, I have *no money*.

23. True/False

    I have had a savings account most of my life.

24. An organized, regular savings plan is
    a. essential to present and future financial security.
    b. a nice idea, yet unrealized in my experience.
    c. too much trouble.
    d. something I started as a child.

25. True/False

    I tithe.

26. True/False

    Giving to charity is important to me.

27. True/False

Conspicuous consumption is not negative.

28. For holiday or birthday gifts for my relatives or my spouse's relatives, we should spend
     a. as much as we can afford.
     b. nothing, just send a card or call.
     c. $25–$50.
     d. $50–$100.
     e. $100–$200.
     f. over $200.

29. True/False

I have bought or would buy stock in a company because I got good vibes.

30. True/False

I have made money in the stock market.

31. True/False

I have lost money in the stock market.

32. True/False

    I haven't invested yet, but I want to.

33. True/False

    I frequently lend money to friends or relatives.

34. True/False

    I can see borrowing a lot of money to start a business of my own someday.

35. True/False

    New is always better than used.

36. Your mother-in-law buys an entire summer wardrobe for your one-year-old daughter. You

    a. return it to her—you don't take charity.

    b. you thank her profusely and pop your baby into her new swimsuit.

    c. accept it, but put it in the bottom drawer.

    d. return it to the store for cash.

37. Of the total family income, I expect to make

    a. 100 percent.

    b. 75 percent.

    c. 50 percent.

    d. 25 percent.

    e. 0 percent.

38. True/False

I believe expensive jewelry and art are investments.

39. True/False

I write a budget each month and adjust it as necessary.

40. True/False

I write a budget each month and rarely deviate from it.

41. True/False

I think debtors' prisons were a good idea.

42. True/False

Declaring bankruptcy has its advantages; if financing things got really bad for us, I can see declaring bankruptcy.

43. A premarital agreement

    a. foreshadows divorce.

    b. bespeaks suspicion and mistrust.

    c. represents a good business decision for both parties.

44. True/False

You get what you pay for.

45. True/False

I believe in paying people to do menial but necessary tasks: shoveling snow, mowing the lawn, etc.

46. Stereo equipment should cost

    a. nothing; we don't need one.

    b. under $175—a boom box is just fine.

    c. $200–$600.

    d. $600–$1,200.

    e. more than $1,200.

    f. whatever it takes to have the best sound system.

47. True/False

Upgrading my stereo system every two years is vital to my mental health.

Has anyone, other than that little pickpocket at the bus station, taken money out of your purse or wallet without asking? If the person was a child, I am sure a scolding was in order. If the person was your beloved, I am sure an argument was in order. Perhaps not. I admit to not knowing the depths of your pockets or your patience.

Let me ask you another question: What do you respect about your soon-to-be-spouse? If you spell respect M-O-N-E-Y or any of its derivatives, such as J-O-B or T-I-T-L-E, imagine finding your spouse waxing the car one Tuesday afternoon because Tuesday morning he or she had become suddenly unencumbered with the rigors of employment. If pulling together heretofore meant pulling up to the bank in your Lexus and pulling cash from your joint account, you may be thinking of pulling up stakes.

It all goes back to what you agree is substance and how you define quality of life. What are you willing to contribute, figuratively and literally, to the joint account? At the heart of most money arguments is the unspoken suspicion that one of you—the other one—is so irresponsible as to spend or mismanage you both into the poorhouse.

Of course, neither one of you wants that, so open those records, put your past-due notices, earnings, savings, and investments on the table next to your hopes, fears, dreams, and expectations. Be embarrassed, be surprised, be relieved, be whatever, but be honest. After the financial revelations are over, your mutual trust stock should be up, and maybe that's what you really need to see you through a rainy day.

13 HOUSECLEANING: FETISH OR FOOLISH?

A "clean" house. How do you define it? Is the definition open to interpretation, as is the definition of, say, a clean mind? Or in fact is "clean" linked in your beloved's mind to a military standard of precision and bouncing quarters off tightly made beds? I suspect you think you understand your betrothed's need for tidiness or the lack of it. What you may not understand is the impact his or her attitude will have on *your* slovenly or pristine life and on your mental health. Is the neat person a neurotic, uptight, uncreative drone? Is the more causal housekeeper a selfish, inconsiderate, disorganized, health-endangering miscreant? Hard to say. Easy to say, however, is that incompatibility in this area can become a chronic sore point, a daily irritation, which, if left festering, can be fatal.

1. I think household chores should be
    a. done by the maid.
    b. divided equally.
    c. done primarily by the woman.
    d. done by whoever notices something is dirty.

2. I believe housework takes about
    a. 1–2 hours a week.
    b. 2–4 hours a week.
    c. 4–6 hours a week.
    d. more than 6 hours a week.

3. I have washed windows
    a. inside the house.
    b. outside the house.
    c. never.

4. Vacuuming should be done
    a. when the carpet crunches when you walk.
    b. at least 1–2 times a week.
    c. every other week.
    d. whenever the floor needs it.
    e. once a month.

5. The bathroom (toilet, shower, sink) needs cleaning
    a. daily.

    b. once a week.

    c. when the grouting changes color.

6. True/False

    I know how to change a vacuum cleaner bag.

7. Bedsheets need to be changed

    a. after they're stained.

    b. once a week.

    c. every other week.

    d. once a month.

    e. whenever I feel like it.

8. True/False

    I move furniture when I clean.

9. True/False

    I have dusted or washed miniblinds.

10. True/False

    I believe in spring cleaning.

11. True/False

I turn my mattress.

12. True/False

I use furniture polish.

13. Dishes can be left in the sink

a. never.

b. after a party.

c. when someone's sick or on vacation.

d. anytime.

14. For me, waking up to a dirty kitchen is

a. a fact of life.

b. depressing.

c. no big deal.

d. an infrequent occurrence.

15. True/False

I empty my toaster's crumb tray frequently.

16. True/False

    I wash the blade on my electric can opener.

17. True/False

    All my kitchen cabinets are well organized: spices, pots and pans, etc.

18. True/False

    Folding towels correctly for the bathroom or linen closet is important to me.

19. If I come home late and find used dishes and glasses on the coffee table and my spouse in bed, I will think
    a. my beloved is ill and couldn't tidy up.
    b. my beloved was exhausted and couldn't tidy up.
    c. my beloved had a small party and was too bombed to tidy up.
    d. my beloved is a selfish, inconsiderate, disorganized, health-endangering miscreant.

20. If the house is in a disarray not of my own making, I will probably
    a. clean it up and say nothing.
    b. clean it up, complaining, accusing, and castigating as I go.
    c. feel comfortable.

   d. leave it for the messy person responsible.

   e. wait to find out why it looks so bad.

21. Hired household help is

   a. a necessary expense.

   b. an extravagance.

   c. a justifiable extravagance.

22. True/False

Effective dusting can be done with a feather duster.

23. Regularly rearranging one's sock drawer and keeping clothes neatly folded at all times is

   a. anal retentive.

   b. the sign of an organized, efficient mind.

   c. probably a good idea but difficult to do.

Cleanliness is next to godliness = all slobs are sinners. An equation with which I am not entirely comfortable. On the tidiness barometer, 10 being hospital-clean and 0 being a fraternity house, how do you rate? Although I am not at liberty to reveal my own number, suffice it to say when my ex-husband learned his replacement was a neat freak who vacuumed the whole house each day, he said it was the "perfect revenge." (In my own defense, said vengeful husband was also the apple peel spewer of Chapter 1. I digress into the petty morbidities of my own alliances. I apologize.)

If you, a squeaky clean 9, are marrying an I've-only-worn-this-underwear-three-days 2, don't fret. Simply make a long list of specific duties, detailing who does what on which days. And you 2's—if you are lucky and sincerely messy, you will lose the list before it's your turn.

A suggestion for those of you who rated 7–10: If your beloved struggles to cultivate a greater sense of cleanliness by trying to help you with some task, *do not criticize the attempt*, or worse, laugh derisively. Responding to honest effort with sarcasm, criticism, or knee slapping will not nurture a budding neatnik. Trust me on this one—I, for one, will never offer to wash another storm window.

14 INFERIOR DECORATING: THE RISE AND FALL OF THE BEANBAG CHAIR

A room divided: a lavender oriental fan graces pale ocher walls, delicately taunting the cowboy-and-Indian battle scene framed in red metal directly across from it. Tranquility versus carnage. You versus your spouse. A man's home is his castle, but does that mean he casts the deciding vote when it comes to decorating? Men, as you read these words, you may be thinking, "I don't even *care* about decorating—she can do the whole thing!" Although I hesitate to contradict you, many of you are wrong. You may not care in a general sense, but you probably care quite a bit in the specific. Let's check. Do you have any trophies you want prominently displayed? Do you have a lot of beautifully framed pictures of you excelling at the sport of your choice? And ladies, must you have an armoire, no matter how small your bedroom? These questions may be food for thought. Or they may not. Maybe your tastes and your beloved's are similar or at least compatible, and you know that. Or maybe you just *think* you're compatible because each of you is too refined and considerate to say to your beloved what you've actually been thinking since your first date: "Your taste stinks."

1. If I could choose another period of time to live in, I'd live in
   a. medieval times.
   b. the early American West
   c. Victorian England.
   d. the future.
   e. the Fred Flintstone era.
   f. other _____

2. If I could live in another part of the world, I'd live in
   a. Europe.
   b. the Orient.
   c. Africa.
   d. South America.
   e. Antarctica.
   f. New Jersey.

3. I think a home full of antiques is
   a. cold and sterile.
   b. uncomfortable.

    c. impractical.

    d. elegant.

    e. an investment worth a little inconvenience.

4. I think most people who redecorate frequently

    a. are bored and boring—they have nothing better to do with their time and money.

    b. are wisely enhancing the value of their property.

    c. are trying to find themselves.

    d. enjoy it and use it as a creative, self-expressive outlet.

5. People who buy secondhand furniture

    a. have my sympathy but not my respect.

    b. are frugal and wise.

    c. may not have a choice.

    d. are inviting other people's germs and dirt.

    e. are usually tightwads.

6. True/False

Buying furniture is an investment.

7. True/False

My mother let me jump on the furniture and put my feet on the coffee table.

8. Every kitchen must have
   a. a double sink.
   b. a disposal.
   c. a dishwasher.
   d. all of the above.

9. If we fell in love with an older home, the kitchen of which had not be updated, I would
   a. refuse to consider buying it.
   b. plan to sink $10,000 into updating it.
   c. buy it and save up for the remodeling job.
   d. buy it and use the kitchen as it is indefinitely.
   e. Plan to do all the remodeling work ourselves as we can afford it.

10. True/False

I like kitchens with cooking utensils and pans hanging on the walls.

11. True/False

    Plants are an integral part of decorating.

12. True/False

    If we were to move cross-country and had to pay for the move ourselves, we would sell most of the furniture rather than pay to move it.

13. For a silk flower centerpiece for the dining room table, I can see spending
    a. under $10.
    b. $10–$25.
    c. $25–$50.
    d. $50–$100.
    e. over $100.

14. True/False

    All shelves and drawers must be lined.

15. True/False

    I have worked with or want to work with an interior decorator.

16. If given a choice, I would usually eat dinner at home
    a. in a formal dining room.
    b. in a breakfast nook.
    c. standing up.
    d. from a TV tray.
    e. sitting at the kitchen table.

17. True/False

    I have or expect to have a complete set of china, silver, and crystal and use it.

18. True/False

    Every dining room needs a china cabinet.

19. Natural wood accents are
    a. beautiful and rich.
    b. a pain to dust and polish.
    c. in need of being painted over immediately.
    d. environmentally unsound.

20. True/False

I want my collections displayed.

21. True/False
    I think pictures of the family make wonderful wall decorations.

22. When I see religious statues, pictures, etc., in other people's homes, I think
    a. how pious they are.
    b. how tasteless they are.
    c. who cares?—it's their house.
    d. this is embarrassing.
    e. this is idolatrous.

23. The kitchen floor should be
    a. wood.
    b. tile.
    c. carpeting.
    d. linoleum.

24. True/False
    I think most decorating projects can be handled by the two of us.

25. True/False

    I prefer hardwood floors to carpeting.

26. When I see radiators in a house, I think
    a. how quaint.
    b. what are these things?
    c. what a pain in the neck.
    d. I bet these people freeze.
    e. how cozy.

27. True/False

    Bare walls depress me.

28. True/False

    Ideally, one room in the house will have something dead mounted on the wall.

29. If there's an extra room in the house, I expect we'll make it
    a. a shared office with a pullout couch.
    b. a guest room.
    c. a den or a TV room.

    d. a storage room.

30. To be a real home, a house must have a

    a. fireplace.

    b. piano.

    c. swimming pool.

    d. two-car garage.

    e. roof.

31. A good number of bathrooms for a family dwelling is

    a. 1.

    b. 2.

    c. 3.

    d. 4 or more.

32. Living room furniture is meant to be

    a. admired and preserved.

    b. used daily.

    c. an investment.

d. able to withstand the slings and arrows of outrageous family living.

33. Beanbag chairs are appropriate
    a. nowhere.
    b. in a playroom or a TV room.
    c. in a living room.
    d. in a bedroom.

34. True/False
    If I had the money, I'd like to mirror the ceiling in the bedroom.

35. My favorite colors for the home are
    a. earth tones.
    b. vibrant colors.
    c. white and black.
    d. pastels.

36. A large entertainment center should go in
    a. the TV room.
    b. the den.

    c. as many rooms as possible.

37. True/False
    I like bathtubs with clawed feet.

38. True/False
    I'd rather have a shower than a tub.

39. Showers should have
    a. glass doors.
    b. sliding glass panels.
    c. shower liners and curtains.
    d. shower liners serving as curtains.

40. True/False
    All towels in the bathroom should be coordinated.

41. True/False
    I expect the color of the appliances in the kitchen to match the decor.

42. True/False

I would like a fur bedspread.

43. True/False

I like waterbeds.

44. True/False

I want a mantelpiece.

45. True/False

I have a need to display bronzed baby shoes.

46. True/False

Eventually, I want a canopy bed in one of the bedrooms.

47. Our bed should be

a. a waterbed.

b. a king or queen.

c. orthopedic.

d. on sale.

Requiring your family to enter their own home through the back door seems inhospitable somehow. Not being allowed to walk, sit, or breathe in certain pristinely elegant rooms does not enhance family members' self-esteem, as it places them a poor second to the house's important tenants: the loveseat, the Tiffany lamps, the baby grand, and the carpet.

Is this to say you should not cherish beautiful things? Certainly not; my antique-collecting pater would shudder at such philistine advice. I caution you, however, to consider what makes a home: tangibles or intangibles? If you similarly define "home" as an atmosphere of warmth created by mutual respect, support, and affection, you can easily weather an occasional tiff over an occasional table. However, if acquisition and redecoration are obsessions, a satisfying sense of home may prove elusive.

I am reminded of a husband of mine who perspired through a stifling afternoon in a Santo Domingan courtroom with a prominent U.S. lawyer's wife, also there for a speedy divorce. As they left the judge, my now ex-husband asked her what she intended to do with her time since the divorce proceedings were concluded. She answered with obvious enthusiasm that she looked forward to completing a yearlong project near and dear to her heart. Knowing her resources and position, he imagined her organizing a gala fund-raiser or establishing an inner-city daycare center or health facility. He should have imagined her knee-deep in tiles and Turkish towels, supervising the redecoration of the master bath, soon to be glorified with skylight, sauna, and massage table. Who said the unexamined life is not worth living?

15 SHOULD AULD ACQUAINTANCE BE FORGOT?

Wouldn't it be fun to see who your spouse-to-be had a crush on in the fourth grade? Imagine those stolen glances on the way to the drinking fountain, those amorous whispers on the playground. Who was it? Probably somebody with freckles, curly hair, and no chest. Alas, maybe that little fourth grader doesn't even have a name anymore in your honey's memory bank. (My crush was on the swarthy fourth grader Marc Goldman—or Mark Goldfarb or Mack Goldstein . . .) Why is it we can chuckle tolerantly about grade school and junior high affairs of the heart and yet find so little humor in a friendly call to our beloved from a grown-up ex-flame? Ah, the road to the altar and beyond is littered with broken hearts. Actually, the brokenhearted are not usually the problem—it's the malingerers, those who hope for just one more smile, one more date, one more civil conversation with your beloved so they can justify waiting another five years, hoping your divorce is right around the corner. These individuals are sometimes hard to recognize because they often lurk among us, disguised as the most revered human beings of all—*true friends*. Woe be unto you if you besmirch the name of your partner's "true friend" by suspecting anything more than a platonic relationship.

1. True/False

    There is no such thing as a "true friend" of the opposite sex.

2. True/False

    All heterosexual relationships have an element of sexuality.

3. If I come home and find my spouse talking on the phone to an old romantic inter-est, I will probably

    a. get on the phone to say "Hi."

    b. get on the phone to say "Blow off."

    c. wait until the conversation is over, then make as many snide and sarcastic remarks as possible before the fight starts.

    d. immediately call an old flame of my own.

    e. do nothing—it's not that big a deal.

    f. express mild interest.

4. A person your spouse almost married is coming through town and wants to meet your beloved for drinks—*alone.* You

    a. have no objection.

    b. say you have no objection but follow them.

    c. make a hot date for yourself.

    d. encourage your spouse to invite the interloper to the house so you can meet each other.

    e. suggest the meeting be held with you present.

    f. demand that the meeting be held with you present.

5. The appropriate amount of time one can spend on the phone with an old friend of the opposite sex is

    a. 10 minutes for every year you haven't seen each other.

    b. unlimited.

    c. none.

    d. until one's spouse wants to use phone or feigns wanting to use phone.

    e. until one's spouse pushes the button.

6. True/False

Former romantic interests do not make suitable business partners.

7. Old friends of the opposite sex can be visited with in person

    a. anytime.

    b. never or infrequently.

    c.   once or twice a year.

    d.   whenever they suggest it.

    e.   whenever you want to start trouble.

8. "Going out with the boys/girls" should happen

    a.   spontaneously.

    b.   once or twice a week.

    c.   once or twice a month.

    d.   rarely or on special occasions only.

9. True/False

To me, "out with the boys/girls" may mean barhopping, drinking, and dancing.

10. True/False

A night out with the boys/girls may mean going to watch members of the opposite sex disrobe to musical accompaniment.

11. At the dinner table, your beloved mentions lunch was had with an ex-"friend" of the opposite sex; a spontaneous type of thing—they just ran into each other. You react by

    a.   sobbing and vomiting.

b. asking how the person is and going on to a subject that actually interests you.

c. attacking, preferably with sarcasm, the morality of both your spouse and the friend.

d. jumping up from the table and refusing to talk until your mate promises to never speak to anyone of the opposite sex again.

e. asking how your spouse felt about the meeting.

f. throwing your least favorite food on the plate at your mate.

Well, what answer did you come up with? Should auld acquaintance be forgot, and, by the way, how auld is auld? For that matter, should new acquaintance be forgot when you are married?

Honesty is the key. I have had a dear friend for seventeen years (eighteen if you count the year we weren't speaking). He is funny, intelligent, creative, supportive, and attractive, but our days of romance ended sixteen years ago. Any person I am involved with knows Rod comes with the territory.

If we are honest with our ourselves, we know a true friend from an old flame. And if we are not honest with ourselves, our spouses are there to help. Remember, they are not unschooled in the nuances of flirtation. Your beloved undoubtedly employed the lowered eyes, the furtive glance, or my personal favorite, the smoldering gaze, to ignite your own passion. Consequently, the stuttered word, the flushed cheek, the glittering eyes all speak of your more-than-platonic interest in an old friend.

Maybe you think it would be exciting somewhere down the marital road to take a detour to fan a few embers. Maybe you think an old flame might even warm up your marriage. Don't buy it. If you do, chances are, before you know it, you will have burned your own house down, no survivors.

16 Children: Babes (a) in Toyland, (b) in the Woods, (c) From Hell

Does the thought of spit-up on your shoulder disgust you? Do you think babies sometimes soil their diapers out of spite? Did you hate babysitting? Did you pull the wings off butterflies? It doesn't matter; you still may be one of the greatest parents in the world. The operative word here is "one," and agreeing on what's best for little Osgood is one of the longest, hardest tests you'll ever take.

1. During your first year of marriage, you find you are going to be parents. You are
   a. overjoyed.
   b. insisting on an abortion.
   c. considering an abortion.
   d. going to quit work.
   e. going to have to get a second job.
   f. going to have to drop out of school.
   g. going to hop the next plane out of town.

2. A wife should quit working
   a. after the doctor confirms the pregnancy.
   b. at about 6 months.
   c. after her water breaks
   d. not at all.

3. No intercourse after
   a. the doctor confirms pregnancy.
   b. the 4th or 5th month.
   c. the 7th or 8th month.
   d. What does that have to do with anything?

4. I like names like
   a. Carol, Jane, Mary, Robert, John, Peter.
   b. Christina, Melissa, Stephanie, Alexandra, Brooke, Clayton, Stone, Drew.
   c. Springbreath, Moonunit, Bladegreen.

5. The nursery should be
   a. completely finished before the baby arrives.
   b. at least planned before the baby arrives.

    c. given no thought until the baby arrives—it's bad luck.

    d. in our bedroom.

6. Breastfeeding is

    a. most desirable.

    b. not necessary.

    c. a good way to ruin your figure.

    d. not desirable.

    e. absolutely out of the question.

7. Bottles with those little collapsible bags inside are

    a. no good.

    b. just fine for daily use.

    c. to be used only on special occasions, travel, etc.

    d. too expensive.

    e. bad for the environment.

8. When they cry, newborns should be

    a. fed.

    b. checked.

    c. ignored if they're dry and have been recently fed and burped.

    d. held and rocked until they calm down.

    e. ignored.

9. Newborns can be left with a babysitter (not a relative)

    a. immediately.

    b. at 4–8 weeks.

    c. at 9–16 weeks.

    d. at 4–5 months.

    e. at 6–8 months.

    f. at 9–10 months.

    g. at about 1 year.

10. A mother should return to work during her child's

    a. infancy.

    b. elementary school years.

    c. junior high years.

    d. high school years.

    e. college years.

11. When the baby cries at 2 A.M., the person who gets up is
   a. Mother.
   b. Father.
   c. Mother and Father.
   d. whoever's shift it is.

12. If a child misbehaves, he/she should be
   a. spanked.
   b. sent to his/her bedroom.
   c. deprived of certain favorite foods.
   d. restricted from favorite activities.
   e. reasoned with.

13. At meals the child should
   a. eat everything—or almost everything—on the plate.
   b. be allowed to choose what will go on the plate, then be made to eat it all.
   c. be allowed to eat whatever he/she chooses.

14. Sweets—candy, cookies, cakes, etc.—should be
   a. a normal part of a child's daily diet.

    b. primarily for special occasions.

    c. allowed rarely.

15. Your 6-year-old child takes a piece of candy or a box of crayons out of a store without your knowledge. You discover the "crime" when both of you have returned to the car in the parking lot.

    a. You make the child return with you to the store and replace the item.

    b. You make the child return with you to the store and apologize to the clerk or manager.

    c. You tell the child never to do it again and leave.

    d. You spank the child in public and make a scene.

    e. You spank the child at home.

    f. You punish in another, noncorporal manner.

16. Children should have

    a. an allowance based on their doing chores.

    b. an allowance—no requirements.

    c. chores—no set allowance.

    d. no specific chores, no allowance.

17. The age children should be allowed to choose all their own clothes is
    a. earlier than 4.
    b. 5–6.
    c. 7–9.
    d. 9–12.
    e. 13–15.
    f. when they pay for them.

18. When a parent is not home during the day and early evening, teenagers should be allowed to entertain
    a. no one.
    b. a same-sex friend.
    c. anyone—4 kids or fewer.
    d. anyone, any number.

19. At 16, a teenager should get a car of his/her own
    a. under no circumstances.
    b. if the teenager buys it with his/her own money.

    c. with the parents' financial help.

    d. from the parents.

20. I expect my child to leave home

    a. at 18 for college.

    b. at 18 to work.

    c. after college.

    d. no set time.

    e. never.

21. If my daughter gets pregnant, I'll

    a. figure it out then.

    b. expect her to keep it.

    c. help raise it.

    d. encourage her to give it away.

    e. encourage her to have an abortion.

22. True/False

High schoolers should have a part-time job.

23. If my child goes on to college, the tuition and expenses will be paid for by
     a. my spouse and me, no strings attached.
     b. the student and us.
     c. scholarships and the student only.
     d. my spouse and me, as a loan.

A prerequisite to having children should be the ability to recite fifteen nursery rhymes in your sleep. As my two-year-old daughter would gently remind me as I started to drool and snore while rocking us both to sleep, the story is about doggies and kitties, not about a darkly handsome young man named Carlos.

Yes, being a role model for the rest of your life is a demanding assignment. That is why all your patterns of behavior must be scrutinized to see if they are worthy of emulation. That is why you must discuss now, prebaby, such issues as your rate of speech. Let me explain its importance by way of example. My wonderful daughter, Alyson, was slower to speak than Grandma Thelma's little neighbor, Dana, who, at age one, spoke like Demosthenes, postpebbles. Aly's father was convinced Aly could not keep up with the Joneses because I spoke so quickly that she could not ascertain where one word ended and the next began. His admonishments did little for my budding maternal psyche. Miraculously, however, Alyson did eventually speak and now talks as fast as I do.

The point of all this is that I believe we are so intent on rearing the perfect child, we forget that little Baby X is actually always learning from us, even as we bicker about the direction the car seat should face and whether letting Baby have the sucker proffered by the grocery checker is the first step toward baby tooth rot and eventual dentures.

Maybe all we can hope is that our children see us gradually giving up our own childishness without losing our childlikeness or our appreciation of theirs.

17 Mentioning the Unmentionables: Religion and Politics

"Swear to God." Is this a figure of speech, one step up from "stick a needle in my eye and hope to die"? Or is it a sacred oath with eternal overtones?

Do you think the Democrats have a wonderfully appropriate symbol in the donkey? Are political parties part of the problem or the solution? Is Washington, D.C., a vibrant international city that radiates power and energy, or is it a seamy metropolis full of back-stabbing (figuratively and literally) opportunists, many of whom are pandering to the military-industrial complex?

1. To me, the military
    a. should be more appreciated because they work hard to preserve our freedom.
    b. is a little scary in their we-know-best attitude
    c. is never anything I think about.
    d. is okay.

2. As far as the military budget goes, I say

    a. who cares?

    b. it is grossly (in every sense of the word) inflated.

    c. we should give them everything they ask for because they know better than we how much it costs to defend this country.

3. True/False

    I believe most politicians have, at one time or another, taken a bribe or have been influenced by wealthy contributors.

4. True/False

    I have worked for or contributed to a national campaign.

5. I vote

    a. in national elections.

    b. in national and local elections.

    c. if I have time.

    d. never.

6. True/False

    All politicians are alike; the party doesn't matter much.

7. In general, Democrats are
   a. bleeding-heart liberals, intent on giving money away.
   b. compassionate, soul-searching and solution-oriented.
   c. about the same as Republicans in my book.

8. True/False
   In political discussions, I have pretended to agree with people to avoid an argument.

9. One thing that could turn me against a candidate is finding out the candidate is
   a. pro-choice.
   b. against abortion.
   c. a homosexual.
   d. in favor of mandatory busing.
   e. a minority-group member.
   f. a woman.
   g. in favor of a tax hike.
   h. in favor of the death penalty.
   i. divorced or had an affair.

    j.   a draft dodger.

    k.   none of these; have to take on an individual basis.

10. Environmental problems should be solved primarily

    a.   at the individual and local level.

    b.   at the state level.

    c.   at the federal and international level.

    d.   all of the above.

11. If I had been alive during the Civil War, I would have fought

    a.   on the Union side.

    b.   for the Confederacy.

    c.   for nobody—I would have gone to Canada.

12. True/False

I have participated in or would participate in a demonstration.

13. True/False

I condone civil disobedience.

14. True/False

    In general, I think the government funds too many social programs for the poor.

15. I think our action in Vietnam was
    a. justifiable and honorable.
    b. a national disgrace.
    c. a game for the Washington warlords.
    d. a bad idea only because we lost.
    e. I really don't have an opinion because I don't have enough facts.

16. True/False

    For the most part, poor people are poor because they choose to be.

17. Republicans are
    a. fiscally responsible and growth-oriented.
    b. slick, rich businessmen out to make a buck at the expense of the taxpayers, the poor, and the environment.
    c. the only ones concerned with adequate national defense and keeping America strong.
    d. warmongers.

18. As a president, Ronald Reagan was
    a. a fine statesman and a good leader.
    b. well intentioned.
    c. Nancy's puppet.
    d. out of his league.
    e. out of his mind.
    f. photogenic and personable.
    g. the embodiment of everything wrong with our political system.

19. The religion I was introduced to as a child taught me
    a. nothing—we didn't go to any church.
    b. God is good and I am good.
    c. God loves and punishes and I deserve both.
    d. heaven and hell are physical locations.
    e. Adam and Eve were real people.
    f. one day we'll all be back on earth with our material bodies intact.

20. When I attended church or Sunday school as a youngster, I found it
    a. stimulating and thought-provoking.

b. comforting.

c. a boring waste of time.

d. illogical.

e. frustrating.

21. True/False

My religion taught me that men rightfully have the last say in important household decisions.

22. As we get older, I expect the amount of time and thought I give to church and spiritual activities to

a. increase.

b. decrease.

c. stay about the same.

23. I expect our children, if we have them, to be raised

a. in our religion.

b. in my spouse's religion.

c. in my religion.

    d. in no formal religion, because beliefs are individual and shouldn't be forced upon you by some denomination.

    e. in both religions—I'll take them to my church one week and my spouse will take them to another the next.

24. I believe the Bible

    a. is completely true—every word of it.

    b. is the history of the Jewish people.

    c. has inspired parts and man-made parts.

    d. is a nice storybook.

    e. is a guide or our lives.

    f. I don't know.

25. I want to worship with my spouse

    a. more than three times a week.

    b. 1–2 times a week.

    c. once a month.

    d. 2–3 times a year.

    e. rarely if ever.

26. If our children leave the faith they've been raised in, I'll
    a. be very disappointed and hurt.
    b. feel I've failed.
    c. applaud their independence.
    d. be angry.
    e. base my reaction on what they *do* choose to believe in.

27. True/False

    I have acted more interested than I actually was in my betrothed's religion because I thought it was good for the relationship.

28. True/False

    I like to talk about God and spiritual subjects.

29. True/False

    Strong religious beliefs provide the foundation for all aspects of life—thoughts, actions, and goals.

30. I believe that when we die
    a. we are united with the people we really loved in our lifetime.
    b. that's all folks—blotto.

c. we are reincarnated.

d. I don't know.

e. we go to heaven.

f. we come back to earth on Judgment Day.

g. we become completely spiritual and maintain our identity but lose our materiality.

Finding someone who can do a good chicken imitation is not easy, but fortunately, I found such a person at a marathon volunteer effort for the politician of our mutual choice. Destiny had surely brought us together—at least for a few hours. Unfortunately, at the end of our wild evening of clucking and stuffing, a bus took him back to Wisconsin and I never saw him again. I berated myself for months, feeling I should have made more of our obvious meeting of minds and sharing of barnyard sounds.

But life was to teach me, three times, that coordinate political views do not necessarily a happy union make. This was a difficult lesson to learn, because I was almost certain they did, particularly when marriage candidates also professed an interest in religion. Later I discovered their interest in religion was marginal, and their interest in *my* religion was nonexistent, contrary to what they had originally professed with all the fervor of new converts.

Faking religious or atheistic zeal, depending which will hasten your steps to the altar, is a poor idea. True feelings have a nasty way of surfacing at the most inconvenient times, such as baptisms, funerals, and Sunday school.

Respect and honesty are once again the issues. If your religious beliefs differ, discuss compromises that may need to be made now as well as those that will definitely need to be made when you have children. If your political views differ, discuss separate vacations around election time.

Mentioning the unmentionables of politics and religion is not an option when you are planning to marry; it is a necessity. Trusting each other with your deepest thoughts and respecting each other's beliefs has to be a little taste of heaven.

THE UPSHOT

There, that wasn't so bad, was it? You've taken the quizzes and know now what makes you so blissfully compatible. You also know where your compatibility suffers glaring breaches.

Now you must decide what course of action you will take when differences of opinion surface over, for example, television programs. Will you simply smile and say, "How 'bout them Cubs?" when you'd prefer to be watching ballet on another station? (You are to be commended if you feel divergent viewing preferences are mere ripples in the pool of your love and nothing to make waves over.)

Maybe you will choose a quiet time later to discuss with your spouse the virtues of compromise and watching anorexics in tutus. Or perhaps you will start saving resolutely toward the purchase of another television so minor squabbles can be averted.

On the other hand, you may choose none of these solutions. As the memory of these enlightening little tests fades, you may opt for the most fruitless of all choices: nagging.

To nag or not to nag—that is the question. Actually, would that it were the question. Rarely do we make a conscious choice to sound dictatorial. We believe we are offering "helpful suggestions" or "gentle reminders." But of course, these are euphemisms; we are nagging.

The trick is to stop the moment before the naggee determines you, the nagger, are metamorphosing into a complete scold and tells you to shut up or worse. Why can nagging so easily lead to an argument? And why is the urge to nag second only to the urge to procreate?

It is simple. We believe we are almost always right. Sharing our wisdom is an act of supreme love and should be received as such. How can our thoughtful proddings be so misunderstood and so maligned?

Not surprisingly, our sweetheart is equally certain of his or her own infallibility. Ah, there is the rub. How can we keep our own self-respect if we heed so many suggestions, however well intentioned? Isn't that the perfect way to encourage the nagger to continue to foist opinions onto us, willy-nilly?

What we are questioning here is the reasonableness of trying to remake our spouse in our own image. This pursuit is not necessary if we respect and like whom we are marrying.

Honestly, do you think your relationship needs major revisions for you to be happy? Have either of you promised to change a personality trait or habit *after* you are married?

Love makes all of us believers, naive and simple, willing to base our futures on the transforming power of love and the ability of tigers to change their stripes. Glory be, sometimes people do change, but more often they do not. So decide what you can and can't live with based on the experiences you've already had.

Some of you who are young and easygoing may be thinking you have absolutely nothing to worry about because anything your beloved does is fine. Your opinions aren't really that strong, so what will there be to nag about?

In my case, I thought I just had an extremely pleasant, flexible attitude. In reality, I had no attitude, no opinion, no person. I had done an excellent job of adapting to everyone else's expectations of what a nice person said and did. When, during my first marriage, I began to have more self-confidence based on my professional life and motherhood, I began to voice opinions that differed from my husband's. He did not care for the change. I did.

Based on my experiences, I offer this advice to you for whom I have such high hopes and good wishes: Know, respect and love yourself—your abilities, your values, your talents, your potential. Be honest with yourself about recognizing who you are, what you are worth, and what you want most in life. When you truly know yourself as a complete person who can stand alone but does not choose to, marry your dearly beloved, and may you both always remember that the strength of your union depends on your strength as individuals.

Closing Note

Readers:

Do you know something I don't? Actually, I suspect you know a great many things I don't, but that fact aside, are there any little things about your own beloved that have surprised, delighted, or appalled you and can be shared with the general public? If so, please send your thoughts to me at:

P.O. Box 55538
Omaha, NE 68155

ABOUT THE AUTHOR

Susan Adams has been a corporate consultant for fourteen years, conducting business-writing seminars throughout the United States. She has also taught English as a Second Language to foreign students at Creighton University and the University of Nebraska at Omaha. Currently she is working on the sequel to *The Marital Compatibility Test*.